How Mexican Immigrants Made America Home

How Mexican Immigrants Made America Home

ASH IMERY-GARCIA

rosen publishing's
rosen central®
New York

A mis abuelos, Irma y Carlos Imery, eres parte de todo lo que hago.

Published in 2019 by The Rosen Publishing Group, Inc.
29 East 21st Street, New York, NY 10010

Library of Congress Cataloging-in-Publication Data

Names: Imery-Garcia, Ash, author.
Title: How Mexican Immigrants Made America Home / Ash Imery-Garcia.
Description: New York : Rosen Central, 2019. | Series: Coming to America: The History of Immigration to the United States | Includes bibliographical references and index. | Audience: Grades 5–8.
Identifiers: LCCN 2017044351| ISBN 9781508181323 (library bound) | ISBN 9781508181330 (pbk.)
Subjects: LCSH: Mexican Americans—History—Juvenile literature. | Immigrants—United States—History—Juvenile literature. | Mexico—Emigration and immigration—History—Juvenile literature. | United States—Emigration and immigration—History—Juvenile literature.
Classification: LCC E184.M5 I4525 2019 | DDC 973/.046872—dc23
LC record available at https://lccn.loc.gov/2017044351

Manufactured in the United States of America

On the cover: Two dancers perform at a Cinco de Mayo celebration.

CONTENTS

Introduction

This nineteenth-century lithograph shows Mexican peons at work in the field as they are supervised by a foreman. During this period, many Mexicans were forced to work on the land of Mexico's wealthy elite in order to pay off debt.

VISA

UNITED STAT

Descended from the indigenous people living in the Americas before colonial rule, Mexican immigrants and Mexican Americans have helped shape the culture and economy of the United States since the early nineteenth century. Their role in the formation of America's identity is complex, marked by waves of economic crises and political strife. Periodically welcomed across the border as a source of inexpensive labor, Mexican immigrants have also been shunned when the political climate deemed them unprofitable.

The impact of Mexican American culture is present in almost every facet of life in the United States. The American landscape is adorned by cities and street names with Mexican origins, particularly in the Southwest, where the land once belonged to Mexico. Mexican

food is incredibly popular and has altered American cuisine with its many hybrid variations. Spanish can be heard across the United States and is the most spoken language after English. According to the US Census Bureau, Spanish instruction classes have become increasingly popular in American schools, with whites accounting for nearly two-thirds of non-Latino Spanish speakers. Influential Mexican American writers, musicians, and artists are informing the tastes of the next generation. Businesses and advertisers have finally started to cater to the needs and desires of a changing American demographic.

Mexican Americans are helping the United States move toward a more multicultural and diverse society. As the world shrinks, America's economy becomes more intertwined with its neighbors, and the national identity has evolved. Mexican immigrants are expanding what it feels like to be an American, how people define themselves, what they look like, and what they choose to remember about their own history.

The Mexican American experience has been marked by racism and turmoil for years. They have been exploited by big business, pushed aside by the educational system, and had their culture stifled by bigotry. After Mexico lost half of its land to the United States, Mexicans in the Southwest suddenly became Mexican Americans. People found themselves labeled as second-class citizens, and they felt unwanted in their homeland. Over the next few generations, Mexican immigrants were denied their civil rights and stripped of their land, and they became the unappreciated backbone of American industry, doing difficult labor for little pay. Even after the civil rights movement of the

1960s and 1970s, Mexicans and Mexican Americans are still considered foreigners who don't quite belong.

Anti-immigrant sentiments paint Mexicans as criminals who cross the border to take resources from Americans. This fails to acknowledge history or see the future as a communal effort. Mexicans have immigrated and stayed in the United States to create new opportunities and because they believe in the promise of a bright American future for all.

The First Mexican Americans

I n the nineteenth century, the majority of the people who lived in Mexico's northern frontier were mestizo, meaning they were descended from a blend of indigenous and Spanish people. When Spanish conquistadors conquered Mexico, they imposed European government, technology, and the Catholic religion upon the indigenous people, but the culture that ultimately arose adopted many elements of native culture. Those in this twice-conquered land, first by Spain and again by the United States in the nineteenth century, would become the first Mexican Americans.

MANIFEST DESTINY AND THE TEXAS REVOLUTION

The first formal interaction between the United States and Mexico was marked by conflict. Mexico gained independence from Spain in 1821 but was entrenched in internal conflict for years to come. Spain made efforts to reclaim power in Mexico until 1836. Meanwhile, the United States had already set its sights on Mexican land in the quest to expand across North America. Manifest Destiny, or the belief that the United States was fated to stretch from coast to coast, greatly influenced the relationship between the two countries. The immense value of the land was matched by the United States' intense desire to acquire it.

In an effort to appease their neighbors, Mexico opened its northern border and allowed American settlers to take up residence in the frontier land. It wasn't long before white settlers came and began to call themselves Texians. The Mexicans and settlers clashed over land ownership and cultural differences. The majority of new settlers failed to abide by Mexico's laws, mainly those that required Americans to convert to Catholicism, pledge allegiance to Mexico, and pay taxes to the Mexican government. Settlers resented Mexican culture and did not want to integrate into a society that they felt was inferior to their own. To make matters worse, after Mexico abolished slavery in 1829, white

settlers, many of whom came from the southern United States, refused to set their slaves free.

In October 1835, these Texians, along with like-minded Mexicans living in the Texas outpost, led a rebellion against Mexico with the intention of forming their own country. This came to be known as the Texas Revolution. Mexico had established a representative federal republic that was led by a president in 1824. However, Antonio López de Santa Anna had dissolved that system in 1834, a year before the revolution began, as a means of dealing with rebel forces around him.

Santa Anna took his soldiers to quell the uprising in Texas. He had suppressed a similar situation in central Mexico the year before and believed that the Texians were simple traitors who could easily be defeated. Mexican troops had initial victories against the Texians, but they were costly and fleeting. In fact, many Mexicans lost their lives in massive frontal attacks, only to have the Texians win the war's critical battles.

Case in point: the Battle of the Alamo. Santa Anna's forces defeated and killed the Texian soldiers. Then, instead of taking time to regroup, Santa Anna pushed his forces forward. Mexican troops were convinced they could secure the Texas border without extra help but were unaware that American soldiers sent by the United States to aid white settlers had begun marching inland toward Mexico City. Santa Anna was captured at the Battle of San Jacinto and signed the Treaties of Velasco on May 13, 1836, in exchange for his freedom. The treaties took Mexican forces out of the region and declared Texas to be an independent nation.

A painting of Antonio López de Santa Anna by Paul Ouvrier. Santa Anna served as Mexico's president and at times dictator periodically from 1833 to 1855.

TEXAS BECOMES THE TWENTY-EIGHTH STATE IN THE UNION

The Republic of Texas existed as an independent country for a decade before it became part of the United States. The majority of Texians had never fully stopped thinking of themselves as American citizens and had supported the annexation of Texas since the beginning of their struggle with Mexico.

On his final day in office, President John Tyler signed an annexation bill that offered to make the Republic of Texas the twenty-eighth state in the Union. His successor, James K. Polk, who had run on a pro-Texas and pro–Manifest Destiny platform, urged the Texians to accept Tyler's offer. In February 1846, Texas officially relinquished its sovereignty to the United States. Because of President Polk's staunch support of annexation, there was reason to believe he had arranged the merger with former president Tyler.

Mexicans saw the maneuver as a slap in the face. Many believed that Texan independence was a farce orchestrated by American politicians to take control of Mexican territory.

While Mexico acknowledged the annexation of Texas, both countries disputed the boundary between Mexico and Texas. Mexico said that the Nueces River separated the two countries, while the United States believed that the border was the Rio Grande. The amount of land each claimed that the United States had acquired was significantly different. After Mexico rejected an offer to sell the disputed territory,

John Tyler served as the tenth president of the United States and signed the annexation bill that offered the Republic of Texas a place in the Union.

US troops moved in and set up camp past the Nueces River. Mexican forces retaliated, and the United States declared war on the basis that Mexico had invaded US territory.

THE MEXICAN-AMERICAN WAR

The Mexican-American War occurred between 1846 and 1848. At this time, many Americans supported Manifest Destiny, but some Americans had opposed the war from the outset. The opposition believed that the conflict was President Polk's personal crusade to expand the country, and slavery, westward.

The Treaty of the Guadalupe Hidalgo, shown here, was signed in 1848 to end the Mexican-American War. It compelled Mexico to relinquish half of its land to the United States.

However, the Democratic Party echoed the people's desire to conquer Mexico in a bid for popularity.

Mexico was unprepared for another war. Mexicans were dispirited and uncertain about the goals of another conflict with the United States, and many Mexican states refused to participate or provide troops to fight invaders. In short time, American soldiers marched into Mexico City and took control of the capital, completing their conquest of Mexican lands east of Texas.

The casualties and repercussions of the conflict were considerable. Both sides agreed to the Treaty of Guadalupe

MEMORIALIZING THE WAR

Lithographs, a type of chemical print made by taking ink impressions with a greased stone or metal, were one of the more popular ways that Americans learned about the Mexican-American War. The images often accompanied printed stories about the conflict in newspapers, books, and pamphlets. Many of these small artworks were hand colored and unique, and they were made with the intention that consumers would purchase the lithographs to hang on their walls at home. Battle scenes depicting American victories were the most popular, and lithographs portraying an idealized vision of combat that featured heroic Americans and passive Mexicans were the most lucrative.

Hidalgo in 1848, which required Mexico to give up roughly half of its land to the United States. The spoils included not only the disputed territory of Texas, but also large portions of the following states: present-day Arizona, New Mexico, Nevada, California, Utah, and Colorado. Although some Americans felt conflicted about the motivations for the war, it was impossible to deny the immense wealth and value of the land itself.

Mexicans living on the land, who numbered at least seventy-five thousand, were given a year to decide if they wanted to leave their homes and go to Mexico or stay and become fully recognized US citizens. Those who remained were promised that their culture, language, and customs would be respected.

Most chose to stay and became the first Mexican Americans in the United States. However, as the border shifted south, the people living in the newly American state became alien in their own home. Mexican Americans needed to learn foreign laws, politics, and social hierarchies. The Treaty of Guadalupe Hidalgo stressed that property rights would be respected, but this was complicated by laws that required specific and often discriminatory criteria for land ownership. And while Catholicism and Mexican customs remained, the predominantly white Protestant majority looked down on Mexican beliefs and thought of themselves as superior. Despite these and other difficulties, Mexican Americans still looked for ways to make a home for themselves in the United States.

VISA

UNITED STAT
OF AMERIC

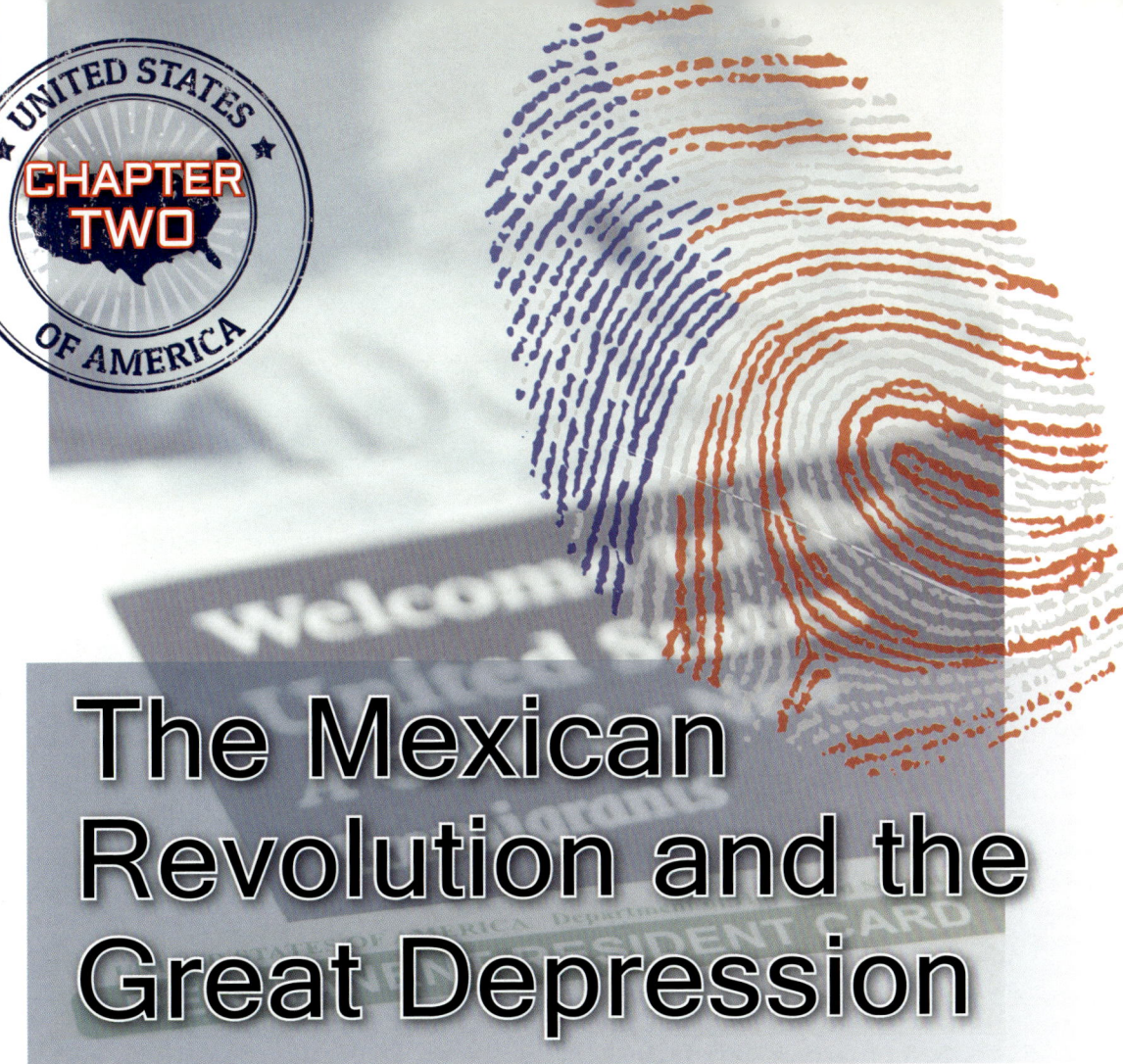

The Mexican Revolution and the Great Depression

eeling from the aftermath of the Mexican-American War, Mexico struggled to accept the loss of land, countrymen, and pride. Many Mexicans viewed not only the United States with distrust, but also their own government. When Porfirio Díaz seized control of Mexico, foreign investors prospered, but small landowners were forced into peonage and labored to pay off their debts. Many indigenous Mexicans lost their land. As more acreage came under the control of

a wealthy elite, the standard of living for Mexicans dropped significantly. With people working for less than twenty cents a day, class tensions peaked and politics became volatile. From 1910 to 1920, many factions fought for power in Mexico. The Mexican Revolution was a period of shifting political alliances and intense violence for the Mexican people.

WORLD WAR I CREATES DEMAND FOR IMMIGRATION

During the decade that encompassed the Mexican Revolution, Mexicans fled the brutality of the conflict and moved north in search of safety and new opportunities. In the midst of this, World War I, a war that never reached the shores of the United States, began in 1914. World War I was a conflict between two massive groups of allies, most of which were European. The United States sided with the French Republic, the British Empire, the Russian Empire, Italy, Japan, and other nations. On the other side were Germany, Austria-Hungary, the Ottoman Empire, and Bulgaria.

The United States increased the amount of agricultural goods it produced in order to supply the Allies. As young Americans left their jobs to join the war, huge swaths of countryside were converted to farmland. That farmland needed workers to cultivate and care for crops. The Mexican Revolution and World War I thus became two events that contributed to a favorable environment for Mexicans to migrate to the United States.

The demographics of those Mexicans who escaped the revolution included people from all social classes. Those who came to the United States with money were able to start Spanish-speaking businesses that catered to Mexican Americans. They became leaders in the Latino communities in the Southwest.

Poor, uneducated refugees had no choice but to take low-paying jobs in agriculture and industry. Displaced Mexican immigrants were recruited along the border to work in the fields of Texas, California, and Colorado. The boom in industrial production also created positions for Mexican immigrants in the iron foundries and coal mines of New Mexico and Arizona. Western railroad construction, an industry previously dominated by Asian immigrants, desperately needed cheap, unskilled labor after Congress curtailed Chinese and Japanese immigration by passing the Immigration Act of 1917.

Two migrants work in Texas's Magic Valley, cultivating mustard greens. Many Mexicans who immigrated to the United States accepted low-paying agricultural jobs in the Southwest.

Working conditions were harsh, and immigrants faced exposure to pollution, long workdays, and injuries. Still, workers preferred the conditions of American work environments to Mexican ones. Thousands moved to the American Southwest with the intention of returning when conditions in Mexico stabilized, but many found comfort and settled in Mexican American communities near the border.

THE GREAT DEPRESSION

The economic prosperity that occurred in the 1920s after World War I spurred a period of reckless economic expansion. People bought stocks at low prices with the intent to sell if their price increased—a process called speculation. At this time, banks also lent unnecessary amounts of money to Americans, and many people bought things on credit.

When the New York Stock Exchange crashed on October 24 and October 29, 1929, stock prices fell drastically, and many people were unable to earn back the money they had invested. More important, those stock prices reflected the value of American businesses, many of which lost almost or more than half of their value.

A vast amount of personal and business wealth disappeared in the crash, and over time the implications of that lost wealth became clear. Businesses and farms slowed production. Many workers were laid off, and those lucky enough to remain employed experienced pay cuts. Families that couldn't afford their loan payments lost their homes as they went into further

THE IMMIGRATION ACT OF 1924

Displaced workers from Mexico were eager to make up for the US labor supply shortage. The need to leave one exploitable group free to enter the country might be why the US government didn't subject Mexican immigrants to the early twentieth century's racist immigration quotas. For example, the Immigration Act of 1924 limited the number of new immigrants to 2 percent of the total for any group already within the United States, according to the 1890 census. The act discriminated against many groups, but it focused particularly on Italians and Eastern European Jews, while effectively stopping the immigration of all Asians to the United States. Mexicans, however, were excluded from any especially limiting restrictions.

Despite any leniency toward Mexicans, the Immigration Act of 1924 reflected increasing fears toward certain immigrant groups that American society treated as undesirable and unable to assimilate into American culture. Union workers in the northern states wanted the act passed and argued that immigrants' willingness to accept substandard pay negatively affected their own earnings.

(continued on the next page)

(continued from the previous page)

Unlike other immigrant groups, most Mexicans lived in the Southwest, away from the reach of northern unions and mostly excluded from American politics. Border security was minimal, and Americans mostly overlooked Mexican migration and focused on Asian immigrants instead. However, the production boom waned between the 1910s and the end of the 1920s, and with it went the importance of Mexican immigrant labor to the American economy.

debt. Banks began to fail as more Americans were unable to make payments. As customers became aware of the crisis, many people demanded their money back. Banks were forced to declare bankruptcy when they didn't have the money customers wanted returned to them.

The collapse of the economy and the ensuing Great Depression heightened tensions between new and old immigrants. As unemployment rose, Americans scrambled to accept any job available, and the influx of cheap labor from Mexico was no longer necessary.

CODED LANGUAGE

Desperate to make sense of an unprecedented event, the American people looked for an easy explanation and a

The New York Stock Exchange on October 24, 1929. Stock prices fell and signaled the beginning of the economic downturn known as the Great Depression.

convenient scapegoat. Now that the country didn't need Mexicans as a labor source like it did during World War I, deep-rooted racism against Mexican immigrants flourished and influenced public policy. In an effort to eliminate foreign job competition, President Herbert Hoover enacted the Mexican Repatriation Program in 1929.

The Repatriation Program was not a law but rather a policy that allowed certain government institutional actors to remove Mexican Americans and immigrants from the United States. It was initially touted as a virtuous endeavor that would strengthen the economy. Instead of stating that the program deported Mexicans, the government discussed the program in terms of repatriating people, or returning them to their homeland. The reality is that probably more than half a million Mexicans—American citizens and immigrants included—were deported from the United States, though there is contention over the exact number. The government fed the American public's worst fears and pushed the idea that the best way to provide jobs for Americans was to get rid of Mexicans and other immigrants.

Program supporters wanted Mexicans deported and neglected to make the distinction between those with US citizenship and those without. Home Relief, the precursor to welfare, cut aid to Mexican families in an effort to lower costs. County agents knocked on doors in Latino neighborhoods with train tickets to Mexico and asked people to vacate by a certain date. Industry titans such as US Steel, Southern Pacific Railroad, and Ford Motor Company pressured their Mexican workers to leave the country by threatening their job security. Local authorities bullied anyone who spoke Spanish or appeared to be of Mexican descent. With the threat of unemployment and the loss of government help, many fled the United States before they could be swept up by the racist onslaught of local agencies trying to coerce

Many Mexican Americans were coerced into leaving their homes and jobs by the local authorities. Freight trains were used to repatriate immigrants back to Mexico.

Mexicans to leave in a way that authorities pretended was voluntary.

Mexicans were shipped across the border in trains and buses. Raids occurred in some states like California, where anyone who appeared to be of Mexican descent could be pulled off the street. And while the majority of these deportations were sponsored by businesses and civic groups, the US government encouraged their actions with racist rhetoric and decided not to intervene to protect its citizens of Mexican descent. Mexico's depressed economy was unprepared to accept the thousands dumped across the border and new economic hardships emerged.

MYTHS AND FACTS

MYTH

Mexicans are lazy.

FACT

The cliché of the lazy Mexican conflicts with the stereotype of Mexicans as people who steal jobs from Americans. In reality, most Mexican immigrants come to the United States looking for employment and often accept the hardest, lowest-paying jobs, which many Americans are unwilling to do. It is false that Mexicans, as a whole, lack a work ethic.

MYTH

Mexican men are violent, aggressive, and prone to criminal activity.

FACT

Gender stereotypes are magnified through the lens of racism. Mexican men, in particular, have been depicted as brutes to justify their mistreatment. In the 1920s, they were depicted as un-American, and that was enough to turn public opinion against them. Such wide-sweeping assumptions are generally not applicable to whole classes of people.

MYTH

Mexican women are docile, family oriented, and hypersexual.

(continued on the next page)

(continued from the previous page)

FACT

When the Spaniards conquered Mexico, their men quickly fraternized with the native women. Likewise, during the conflict with Mexico, American soldiers were quick to comment on the kindness and beauty of the Mexican señoritas, and often imagined that they were the objects of those women's desire.

The stereotype of the beautiful Mexican woman alleviated fears that interracial relationships would threaten the white race. Endowing Mexican women with qualities associated with idealized femininity, such as being submissive and family oriented, allowed white men to feel that they were salvaging the best parts of the Mexican race by having children with Mexican women.

WWII and the Braceros

The United States entered World War II, another global conflict of alliances, after Japanese forces attacked Pearl Harbor on December 6, 1942. As young men made their way to the frontlines, many women chose to enter the workforce and took on financial responsibilities that had been traditionally reserved for men. Despite the rise of working women, there were still many areas of the economy experiencing labor shortages, particularly in agriculture.

BRACERO WORKERS

The labor shortage of World War II meant that the United States couldn't keep up with the demand for greater crop production necessary for the war effort. To counteract this, the US government, in conjunction with Mexico, instituted the Bracero Program in 1942. The word *bracero* stems from the Spanish word *brazos*, for arms, and it means someone who works with his hands.

Braceros were manual laborers who traveled from place to place for work and accepted difficult jobs for little pay. Initially a mutually beneficial program, it was incredibly popular with American companies and Mexican politicians. Mexico profited by having a portion of its population working in the United States, and the braceros' meager wages allowed for lower food prices for wartime and postwar consumers. From 1942 until 1962, the braceros signed almost five million labor contracts, and Mexicans clamored for the opportunity to come to the United States.

As Mexico industrialized its own agricultural industry, new technology uprooted and replaced farmers. Unemployment was rampant, and many Mexicans had high expectations about working in the United States. Mexicans sought out bracero recruitment centers, but not everyone was eligible for contracts. Only young men who had farming experience and did not own property of their own were accepted into the program, and only after obtaining written approval from an authority in their local community. Many of these men were going to the United States to work so they could send money back to their families

Bracero workers were recruited along the border and sent to work for American companies in the Southwest, earning meager wages for difficult work.

in Mexico. Although the jobs were difficult, the pay was still more than what they could earn in their homeland and allowed them to provide for their families.

STRICT AND UNFAIR POLICIES

Many Mexicans who did not fit the strict criteria to become braceros migrated across the border without the approval

of the Mexican or US government. Mexican employers panicked because there weren't enough laborers left in Mexico. Meanwhile, braceros already in the United States blamed undocumented workers for declining labor conditions and lower wages.

There was concern that the braceros would remain in the United States after their commitment to American employers ended because Mexico had limited job opportunities. To ensure that braceros would repatriate, Mexico withheld 10 percent of each worker's wages in Mexican banks and promised that they would receive the money once they returned.

Most braceros never received their withheld wages. The majority were illiterate, rural farmers who did not realize that a portion of their pay was being withheld from them. And because employers and government agents buried the caveat in the bracero contracts, even educated Mexicans had a difficult time understanding what they had signed. When many workers discovered they had money waiting for them, it was impossible to collect it.

While bracero contracts guaranteed certain basic benefits, such as housing, food, and medical services, many of these safeguards couldn't be implemented without support from American employers. When benefits were provided, they were often substandard.

Much of the housing designated for workers was pest ridden and insufficient. Braceros lived in run-down farm structures, modified chicken coops, and repurposed railroad cars. The food, available for a price through concessionaires, was of low quality, sometimes rancid, and distastefully foreign

Working conditions for braceros were inhumane, and migrants were expected to work long hours in the fields. The food given to workers was often substandard.

to Mexicans. Working conditions were harsh, and workers often endured physical mistreatment at the hands of their employers, along with racial prejudice and discrimination. Low net earnings were also an issue, with some braceros paying more for room and board than they were able to make in the fields. They were essentially punished for following the law.

Still, workers were easy to find and accustomed to economic servitude after living in extreme poverty in Mexico. Hardworking and not likely to complain about poor working conditions, Mexicans continued to come to the United States

hoping to make enough money to support themselves. And the uptick in immigration included those who had been accepted into the program along with their extended families.

LEMON GROVE INCIDENT

In 1931, school segregation was routine. The construction of a separate school for Mexican children in Lemon Grove, California, was a common injustice that was part of a wider trend. Families in the Lemon Grove school district claimed that Mexican students were creating "amoral and unsanitary" conditions for white students. Without informing Mexican parents, the district used limited funds to construct a separate school for Mexicans. When Mexican families discovered that their children were expected to learn in a hastily constructed two-room *cabaleriza* (a barn), they were outraged and called for a boycott. Each time children were turned away from the schoolhouse door, Mexican parents requested that they return home rather than learn in a substandard environment. The families sued and won. *Roberto Alvarez v. the Board of Trustees of the Lemon Grove School District* was the first successful school desegregation case in the United States.

VISA

UNITED STATES
OF AMERICA

THE US AND MEXICAN GOVERNMENTS CONSPIRE

With the help of the Mexican government, the United States launched an operation to deport Mexicans. In 1954, the operation deported thousands and dropped them off in parts of rural Mexico in need of laborers. The operation had initial support from Mexicans affected by the labor shortage. It also found some initial support from those Mexican American citizens who believed their standard of living was lowered by the presence of undocumented workers in the country.

After the program started, Mexicans and Mexican Americans realized the initiative was not conceived with their best interests in mind. Discrimination and raids became commonplace in the Southwest, and government agents failed to distinguish between undocumented Mexicans and Mexican American citizens. The fear of deportation devastated families and interfered with day-to-day life as raids in Mexican workplaces and communities became routine. Even the US government's name for the operation was offensive: Operation Wetback. ("Wetback" was a widely used racial slur for Mexicans.) Moral issues aside, the operation was ineffective, and many individuals made their way back to the United States after being deported.

Influenced by the civil rights movement, socially conscious organizations and individuals called for reform and argued that the treatment of migrant workers was inhumane. Politicians decided to look more closely at the program's faults. From the perspective of American agribusiness, it was time to explore other sources of labor. The establishment of a $1.00 hourly minimum wage for braceros made legal immigrant labor less attractive to employers. As cheap labor became more expensive and mechanization began to change the economics of growing food in America, bracero employment diminished throughout the 1960s. The bracero program ended in 1964.

The Chicano Movement

The civil rights movement of the 1960s and 1970s drastically changed the Mexican American community. After generations of being excluded from full participation in American life, Mexican Americans began to demand their civil liberties by protesting and participating in intellectual debate during the Chicano movement. The overall goal of these activists was to overcome the systemic cultural and racial prejudice that had shaped Mexican American life since the nineteenth century.

A NEW GENERATION OF LEADERS

The generation of activists and community leaders who began to use the word "Chicano" were on the border of Mexican and American identities. In the past, Mexican American groups had stressed learning English and integrating into American culture through civil service.

Chicanismo was a deliberate step away from being Mexican American, which was seen as too entangled with white America. Overall, the Chicano movement was indifferent to assimilation. It was a movement that urged communities to take pride in their Mexican heritage and encouraged people to speak Spanish, celebrate diversity, and honor traditional customs. Movement leaders argued that Mexican Americans who identified themselves by their job or social class were falling into the trap of labeling each other as an economic commodity, which is how the United States had viewed Mexican immigrants for generations.

Young and radical, Chicanos were also committed to obtaining meaningful political representation and achieving equality for Mexican Americans, particularly in education. Predominantly Mexican American schools had the worst teachers and were overcrowded and severely underfunded. A large number of white Americans viewed the education system as a means to teach the children of immigrants that the only way they could contribute to American society was as a source of cheap labor. Subjected to racism and prejudice from school administrators and teachers, Mexican children were seen as

Chicanos protest against discrimination and racism. The Chicano movement fought for better education and workers' rights, and it sought to give Chicanos a political voice.

intellectually inferior and received a substandard education. The Chicano movement decided to address the issue of education directly, as it was one of their main concerns.

STUDENT WALKOUTS

José Ángel Gutiérrez, Mario Compean, William "Willie" Velásquez, Ignacio Pérez, and Juan Patlán founded the Mexican American Youth Organization (MAYO) in 1967. MAYO played an essential role in mobilizing students for education reform by staging a series of walkouts in and around San Antonio, Texas, to establish Chicano student representation on the school boards.

Despite the large Mexican population in the San Antonio area, the school boards were completely made up of white people, particularly those who were hostile to Mexican economic advancement. Mexican American students were informally segregated because they went to schools with lower funding and faced daily discrimination from their teachers and administrators. San Antonio schools prohibited Spanish, taught a biased curriculum, and did not prepare Mexican American students for college. These were decisions that the all-white school board backed.

Influenced by nonviolent activism and the black civil rights movement, MAYO staged more than thirty-nine walkouts in Texas high schools. Students carried signs reading "Better Education Today—Not Tomorrow" and advocated for their rights to speak Spanish, get a quality education, learn Mexican American history, and attend schools free of discrimination.

José Ángel Gutiérrez, one of the five original MAYO founders, staged walk-outs in Texas schools demanding fair and equal education for Mexican American students.

MAYO struck a chord with adults in their communities. Parents, college students, and clergy came to support the walkouts. Teachers and students alike were suspended for speaking their minds, and the school board refused to meet with student activists to discuss grievances.

Then, in 1968, the newly formed Mexican American Legal Defense (MALD, now MALDEF) filed a lawsuit on behalf of students. MALD alleged that the Fourteenth Amendment rights of the Mexican American students were being violated because of the inadequate education that only they received. MAYO and MALD found success when the court found the school board's policies unconstitutional. MAYO's activism in Texas inspired Mexican American students across the nation to stage their own walkouts.

CHICANA STUDIES

As more Mexican Americans went on to pursue higher education in the 1960s and 1970s, feminism of a Chicana, or female Mexican American, variety emerged alongside the larger white American feminist movement. While women had always had a role in the Mexican American community, they now demanded a voice. In the movement, issues of social and economic inequality still took precedence, but gender and sexuality also became a part of the conversation as Chicanas searched for their own political identity.

Chicanas were instrumental in raising the bar for thoughtful activism. Their primary goals were to acknowledge women's labor and secure their rights to education, employment, and a political voice. Chicanas believed that differences between men and women were socially constructed. They rejected the stereotype of Mexican American women as quiet homemakers and challenged the oppression they faced because of racial, gender, and class discrimination.

Like other facets of the movement, Chicanas celebrated their roots and criticized oppressive traditions. Many parts of indigenous culture were glorified as a more equal way of life corrupted by Spanish conquerors. For example, in indigenous societies, women got married after they had entered adulthood and formed social bonds within their communities. Under Spanish colonial rule, with the Catholic Church's emphasis on chastity, girls were encouraged to marry as young as twelve or fourteen—often to much older men. The drastic age difference, along with strict limitations on female sexuality, changed gender relations and undermined women's autonomy.

AZTLÁN

Aztlán is the legendary home of the Aztecs before the founding of Mexico. Believed by many to have been located in the American Southwest, Chicanos rediscovered the idea of Aztlán in the late 1960s. The Aztec homeland was believed to be far north

(continued on the next page)

(continued from the previous page)

of where we traditionally think of the Aztec Empire, possibly somewhere in present-day New Mexico.

According to legend, the Aztecs left Aztlán at the command of Huitzilopochtli, the Mexican god of war. Huitzilopochtli told his people to leave in search of Tenochtitlán (modern-day Mexico City). Although they settled in Tenochtitlán, the Aztecs always longed to return to their original land.

Huitzilopochtli, the Aztec god of war, was believed to have ordered the Aztecs to leave Aztlán in search of a new home farther south.

Because they were caught somewhere between Mexican and American culture, it was comforting for Chicanos and Mexican immigrants to claim rights to an ancestral home in the United States. Aztlán gave Mexican Americans a sense of pride and belonging even while white America largely saw them as illegals. The existence of Aztlán wasn't as important as what it represented to Chicanos, which was a hopeful future in America.

Chicana intellectuals recognized the importance of history and weren't afraid to connect how Spanish oppression had affected the values of Mexican Americans, just as US imperialism oppressed Chicanos.

THE ACHIEVEMENTS OF CIVIL RIGHTS ACTIVIST CESAR CHAVEZ

The Chicano movement found a national leader in the farmworker strikes in California and Texas. Cesar Chavez, a Mexican American born in Arizona, began working in the

Dolores Huerta and Cesar Chavez founded the National Farm Workers Association in 1962. The pair would work together to help better the lives and wages of farm workers in the United States for years.

VISA

UNITED STATE
OF AMERIC

fields with his family as a boy and went on to become one of the central figures in the agricultural labor strikes of the 1960s.

Cesar Chavez and Dolores Huerta formed the National Farm Workers Association (NFWA) in 1962. Chavez organized strikes and boycotts to gain higher wages for workers and ignited a lasting passion for workers' rights within the Mexican American community. The NFWA figured prominently in the Delano Grape Strike in 1965, a strike that Larry Itliong and the Agricultural Workers Organizing Committee (AWOC) initiated against grape growers to seek higher wages. The NFWA and AWOC merged into the United Farm Workers Organizing Committee (UFWOC) on August 22, 1966. The UFWOC successfully organized a national grape boycott. The result of this strike and boycott was that the UFWOC was rewarded with union representation and higher wages.

Chavez advocated for the rights of farmworkers and publicized the injustices that American agribusiness perpetrated. What started as a localized collective effort eventually grew into a nationwide movement. Cesar Chavez promoted the use of radical nonviolent protest and traveled the country making speeches about the importance of workers' rights. Dolores Huerta, often overlooked in the movement, was instrumental to the union's successes and lobbied alongside Chavez for worker's rights. She coined the phrase "*Sí, se puede*" or "Yes, we can," which has inspired generations of activists.

CHAPTER FIVE

NAFTA and the Criminalization of the Border

I n 1992, Mexico, Canada, and the United States signed the North American Free Trade Agreement (NAFTA). The agreement reshaped the longstanding economic exchange between all three countries, but particularly affected the relationship between Mexico and the United States.

MEXICO'S ECONOMY

When NAFTA was implemented, one result was that it eliminated tariffs between the United States and Mexico. This

caused the Mexican economy to change drastically. Small rural farmers in Mexico couldn't compete with US agribusiness, particularly corn producers who enjoyed American subsidies. Steep competition forced many Mexicans to look for work elsewhere. Corn-producing regions in Mexico, like Chiapas, that had not traditionally participated in migration to the United States experienced an exodus of workers. Poverty hit indigenous populations hard, and many looked for better opportunities across the border.

For those who chose to stay in Mexico, unemployment and organized crime ravaged rural communities. The economic crisis made the narcotics industry one of the most lucrative in Mexico. Farmers unable to compete with US agribusiness began growing marijuana and poppies for the burgeoning drug trade. The cartels recruited the urban poor as foot soldiers and bribed police and military to act as muscle. Free trade increased activity along the border and made it easier to smuggle drugs along with legal products bound for the United States. Weapons from the United States were also easier to smuggle into Mexico and allowed the cartels to militarize.

As crime spilled over into US border towns, American politicians began to discuss the "War on Drugs" and pushed for stronger border enforcement to keep out growing violence. Drug trafficking was treated as a threat to national security, and Mexicans were demonized and associated with criminal activity. In reality, the booming cartel business would never have been possible without American demand.

MILITARIZATION OF THE BORDER

While the United States welcomed the increased trade of physical goods in and out of Mexico, heightened border security made it more difficult for Mexicans hoping to come to the United States. Legal forms of immigration were cut back, and workers faced new challenges entering the United States. The US Immigration and Naturalization Service (INS) began

US Citizenship and Immigration Services (USCIS) is the administrative branch of the former US Immigration and Naturalization Service (INS). The USCIS handles visas, naturalization services, and refugee applications.

setting up blockades and armed officers along the border to prevent undocumented immigrants from crossing.

New legislation increased the INS budget, allowing for more surveillance equipment, fencing, and law enforcement. The United States thought that if Mexicans could be dissuaded from crossing over, less time and money would be spent on apprehending immigrants once they had entered the country. Those not deterred by the increased border security often gave up due to multiple apprehensions or a lack of resources. The true effectiveness of increased border enforcement is hard to measure because it is difficult to say whether Mexicans are truly being deterred from crossing or if undocumented individuals are coming to the United States by other methods.

COYOTES

With the more popular entry points secure, Mexicans began to take more dangerous routes through deserts and mountains to come to the United States. The militarization of the border resulted in a sharp increase in deaths of migrants attempting the journey. With the risks and dangers associated with crossing, more Mexicans turned to coyotes, or smugglers, to gain entry into the country.

Coyotes are paid guides who assist those seeking safe passage to the United States. Coyotes are known for being highly knowledgeable about border security, checkpoints, and new technology, and undocumented migrants often use them the first time they cross the border. It's less likely they will be apprehended if they cross with someone who has made the trip before, although the fee for being smuggled has risen with the risks of the journey. People pay thousands of dollars to coyotes, corrupt border officials, and the Mexican cartels that control routes to the United States.

In some unfortunate cases, coyotes have sold people off to the cartels or abandoned them after collecting their fee. Some coyotes work with the cartels, and migrants might be asked to participate in drug smuggling in exchange for a reduced fee. Typically, the more an individual can pay, the more they are guaranteed easy passage.

STRICTER IMMIGRATION POLICIES

In addition to making it more difficult for Mexicans to immigrate, President Bill Clinton signed into law new policies that criminalized undocumented individuals. The Anti-Terrorism and Effective Death Penalty Act (AEDPA) allowed immigrants to be deported without review if they had committed any crime. This included minor offenses and crimes committed before the law was enacted, meaning some immigrants were deported after they had served their time.

The Illegal Immigration Reform and Immigrant Responsibility Act (IIRIRA) added more hurdles for those hoping to live in the United States. IIRIRA began the construction of a fence along the US-Mexico border and called for double the amount of border patrol agents, more justifications for deportation, fewer documents that could satisfy identity and employment requirements, and a new rule that prevented legal immigrants from receiving government aid for the first five years they lived in the United States.

Tighter border controls have caused many people to prolong their stay in the United States. Some have settled permanently. Many prefer to live illegally in the United States than have to deal with the bureaucracy of reentering the country for work. This can appear as a win for policy makers who see fewer apprehensions at the border. However, those policy makers understand very little about how many undocumented workers are in the United States.

US Border Patrol agents in McAllen, Texas, detain immigrants who have crossed the US-Mexico border. Thousands of families and unaccompanied minors come to the United States seeking asylum.

As the Mexican economy becomes more intertwined with American businesses, it is difficult to tell legal and illegal migrants apart. Border enforcement officials struggle to allow the growing number of legal migrants into the United States, while also attempting to apprehend those without documents. These officials are overwhelmed, and inspectors often have to choose between two opposing objectives: to keep the line moving for legal workers or to control the growing number of illegal migrants.

Often, questions of economy and approach seem irrelevant. How Congress and the public *feel* about border security is often more important than how effective it is in practice.

VISA UNITED STAT

The American Dream

The disconnect between the idealized story of immigration and the reality of the experience is difficult for both native-born Americans and immigrants to reconcile. Often, the same people proud of America's immigrant heritage also support stricter regulations on who is allowed to participate in American life. Many immigrants have found the path to US citizenship to be treacherous and have chosen to stay in the country illegally, despite being shuttered from many of the opportunities that initially drew them to the United States.

VISA

While comprehensive immigration reform has remained elusive for several decades, one initiative that has been able to gain traction is the Development, Relief, and Education for Alien Minors Act, or the DREAM Act.

DREAMERS

Initially introduced to Congress in 2001, the DREAM Act would allow immigrants brought to the United States as children to gain residency status and the chance to attend college. Unlike more complicated issues attached to major immigration reform, the DREAM Act was able to garner support from both Republicans and Democrats by putting a face on undocumented immigration.

Those eligible to become DREAMers are young immigrants, many from Mexico, who were brought to the United States illegally as children. DREAMers faced overwhelming challenges as they reached high school age and prepared to enter college and the workforce. Without the ability to receive federal loans to attend college or the ability to legally work, Latino DREAMers were looking at a future as economically immobile working poor.

In the 1990s, the majority of Americans were against the idea of undocumented immigrants gaining citizenship. They found the idea of granting them education benefits to be an unjust reward for breaking the law.

Many DREAMers are American in character and only remember living in the United States. The narrow focus on DREAMers allowed the public to empathize with young

DREAMers rally in Washington, DC, urging Congress to pass the DREAM Act, which would allow undocumented immigrant students the chance to obtain a college degree and become US citizens.

people trying to learn and contribute to American society. Like the DREAMers, most Americans saw college education as a prerequisite to success. Americans imagined how it would feel to have their own children unable to pursue their aspirations. The idea of subjecting an entire generation of youth to a life of poverty and social strife was unnerving, and even some of those opposed to the DREAM Act expressed sympathy for the DREAMers.

It seemed as though the DREAM Act had the potential to pass, but after the terrorist attacks of September 11, 2001, public opinion soured on the issue. Although the attacks had been committed by foreigners who had entered the country legally, the tone of the conversation around immigration reform shifted. More people began to oppose the DREAM Act. Young DREAMers continued to advocate for themselves, but Congress seemed less likely to pass an immigration reform bill.

In 2012, President Barack Obama initiated Deferred Action for Childhood Arrivals (DACA). DACA was a policy that allowed undocumented immigrants who had come to the United States as children to receive federal deferred action from deportation and allowed them to work in the United States for two years. After the two-year expiration, those eligible could apply for a renewal of their DACA status. Although over half a million individuals have been approved for DACA, the number of young immigrants who qualify is significantly higher.

Of course, while this was good news for DREAMers, laws preventing undocumented students from receiving a college degree were still very much present at the state level, and it seemed as though the window of opportunity to pass the DREAM Act was gone.

Cinco de Mayo celebrates a battle in Puebla, Mexico, against French troops that took place on May 5, 1862. On that date, a small group of mostly indigenous Mexicans defeated an army of nearly seven thousand French soldiers who had invaded Mexico.

Mexican immigrants in California first celebrated the holiday during the Civil War. Cinco de Mayo began as a way to counter racism and give Mexican Americans a sense of pride. The holiday signifies a moment in history in which Mexican mestizos, always the underdog, overcame the odds and won against a better-equipped enemy. To those who participate in festivities, the message of perseverance is clear and gives many Mexican Americans a sense of belonging in a country reluctant to accept them.

Cinco de Mayo has always celebrated being a part of two cultures, as evidenced by the tradition of placing both the American and Mexican flag side by side during the holiday. Celebrations take place all over the United States, with the same familiar elements of fireworks, street food, parades, mariachi music, and dancers. The mood of the holiday is festive and chaotic and has attracted other cultures to join in on the fun. The popularity of Cinco de Mayo indicates a shift in attitudes and culture as Mexican American influence continues to expand across the country.

RECENT POLITICAL TRENDS

At the start of President Donald Trump's administration, many became wary of applying to the program. There were concerns that the administration, which expressed a desire to curtail both legal and illegal immigration, might use the information to find and deport individuals if the president chose to end the program. Suspicions that Trump might want to end DACA stemmed from his 2015 presidential campaign announcement speech. Trump said, "When Mexico sends its people, they're not sending their best. ... They're sending people that have lots of problems, and they're bringing those problems with us. They're bringing drugs. They're bringing crime. They're rapists." In an effort to appeal to his supporters, he also isolated and frightened the Mexican American community.

President Trump delivered on his xenophobic campaign promises. His policies have permitted local police to act as immigration officials capable of stopping people they believe to be in the country illegally. In August 2017, President Trump pardoned former Arizona sheriff Joe Arpaio, who a federal judge ruled had illegally discriminated against Latinos in patrols and used racial profiling in enforcement efforts. On September 5, 2017, President Trump rescinded DACA.

Despite wide grassroots support for immigration reform and a growing number of Mexican Americans in the United States, it appears that stricter laws, not leniency, are the most likely direction for the future of immigration.

Attitudes toward Mexican immigration have differed throughout history, but the United States is becoming more

Activists protest the cancellation of DACA. Many DACA recipients have been left with an uncertain future since President Donald Trump's decision to end the program on September 5, 2017.

multicultural with each generation. According to a Pew Research study from 2014, the Latino population is expected to double to 106 million by 2050, with the majority being of Mexican descent. As the demographics of the United States change, Mexican American issues and values will come to the forefront as Mexican Americans increase in number. As their voting power increases, Latinos are changing the face of the US electorate. As Mexican Americans overcome the social barriers of race and discrimination, they will further enrich and redefine what it means to be American.

MEXICAN AMERICANS

Population

According to the US Census Bureau, about thirty-six million Mexican Americans live in the United States. This is 63.4 percent of the Latino population.

US States with Large Mexican American Populations

California, Texas, and Florida

Major Holidays/Cultural Celebrations

Cinco de Mayo
Día de los Muertos (Day of the Dead)

Cuisine

Traditional Mexican foods such as tortillas, tacos, tamales, enchiladas, and salsas are enjoyed daily by the Mexican American community. Tex-Mex, a blend of Mexican cuisine altered to fit American tastes, includes popular dishes such as nachos, fajitas, burritos, and hard-shell tacos.

Languages Spoken

Spanish and English

Religion

Catholicism

VISA UNITED STATE OF AMERIC

Mexican Americans in Science and Technology

Lydia Villa-Komaroff is an important molecular and cellular biologist and a founder of the Society for the Advancement of Chicanos/Hispanics and Native Americans in Science (SACNAS).

Ellen Ochoa was the first Hispanic woman to go into space. She is currently the director of NASA's Johnson Space Center.

Sarah Stewart conducted groundbreaking cancer research in the field of viral oncology.

Mexican American Artists and Writers

Cecilia Alvarez is a prominent painter and muralist.

Jhonen Vasquez is known for creating comic books and the Nickelodeon television series *Invader Zim*.

Juan Felipe Herrera served as the US poet laureate from 2015 to 2017.

Mexican American Activists

Aurora Castillo, an environmentalist, founded the Mothers of East Los Angeles (MELA) organization.

Alex Pacheco helped start the animal rights movement in the United States.

TIMELINE

1836 The Republic of Texas forms after it wins its independence from Mexico.

1845 The United States annexes Texas and declares it the twenty-eighth state to be admitted into the Union.

1848 The United States and Mexico sign the Treaty of Guadalupe Hidalgo. Mexico cedes half of its land to the United States.

1910 The Mexican Revolution begins.

1914 World War I, a conflict between two large, global alliances, begins. Americans recruit workers from Mexico at the border for agricultural work to assist with the war effort.

1924 The United States enacts the Immigration Act of 1924. It primarily targets immigrants from Asia and limits immigration to 2 percent of the total number of people within a given nationality already within the United States.

1929 The New York Stock Exchange crashes. The start of the Great Depression creates economic and social unrest.

1929 The Mexican Repatriation Program begins to deport both Mexicans and Mexican Americans.

1939 World War II, a conflict between the Allied and Axis powers, begins. During this war, contracted Mexican migrants are brought into the United States to fill open labor positions.

1942 The Bracero Program, in which Mexican migrant workers are contracted to work for US companies for a period of time before returning to Mexico, begins.

VISA

1954 Operation Wetback apprehends and deports thousands of undocumented Mexican migrants and drops them off in rural, underemployed parts of Mexico.

1962 Cesar Chavez and Dolores Huerta form the National Farm Workers Association (NFWA) to advocate for migrant workers' rights.

1992 The North American Free Trade Agreement (NAFTA) is signed and free trade is established between Canada, Mexico, and the United States.

2001 The DREAM Act is introduced in the Senate and advocates for young undocumented immigrants to be able to obtain a college education and have a chance to apply for permanent residency.

2012 President Barack Obama's administration introduces Deferred Action for Childhood Arrivals (DACA).

2017 President Donald Trump rescinds DACA.

agribusiness Businesses in the agriculture or farming industry.

annexation Making a territory into part of a country.

bracero A Spanish word for manual laborer, or one who works with his (or her) arms. It came to mean a Mexican laborer allowed into the United States to work for a period of time in agriculture.

cede To give up power or land to another person, group, or country.

Chicano/Chicana Mexican Americans who exist between Mexican and American identities and believe in celebrating their Mexican roots.

deferred Put off or delayed until a later time.

displaced Forced to leave home, often because of political instability that might result in violence or a natural disaster.

empathize To relate to someone else's position.

foundries Places where metal is manufactured.

Hispanic Of or related to Spain, the Spanish language, or countries where the national language is Spanish.

ideology A set of beliefs.

imperialism When a country extends its power by acquiring smaller or weaker territories.

Latino/Latina In the United States, used to mean a person from or a descendant of people from countries in the Americas where Spanish or Portuguese is spoken. In Hispanic countries, it is used to mean an American descended from Hispanic people.

VISA

UNITED STAT

Manifest Destiny The nineteenth-century belief that the United States was fated to acquire territory all the way to the Pacific coast of the North American continent.

mestizo Someone of mixed Spanish and indigenous descent.

migrant worker Someone who travels from place to place in search of work.

oppressive Unfairly forceful or restrictive.

peonage Economic servitude or slavery.

quota An allowed minimum or maximum.

repatriation The process of returning to one's home country, voluntarily or by force.

scapegoat A person or group who is blamed and often punished for something that has other, perhaps difficult to determine, causes.

segregation The practice of physically separating different races into different spaces.

speculation The practice of investing in stocks and taking on the risk that they may lose value in the future.

FOR MORE INFORMATION

American Civil Liberties Union (ACLU)
125 Broad Street, 18th Floor
New York, NY 10004
(212) 549-2500
Website: https://www.aclu.org
Facebook and Twitter: @aclu
The ACLU works within the legal system to defend the rights
   of individuals that the US Constitution guarantees.

Centre for Spanish Speaking Peoples
2141 Jane Street, 2nd Floor
Toronto, Ontario M3M1A2
Canada
(416) 533-8545
Website: http://www.spanishservices.org/en
Facebook: @CPGHH
The Centre for Spanish Speaking Peoples (CSSP) provides
   legal counsel, medical services, and programs for new
   immigrants trying to adjust to life in Canada. The centre
   also works to end violence against women and teach
   youth how to challenge homophobia in schools and
   youth spaces.

Chicana/Latina Foundation (CLF)
1419 Burlingame Avenue, Suite W2
Burlingame, CA 94010
(650) 373-1083
Website: http://chicanalatina.org/index.php
Facebook: @ChicanaLatinaFoundation

The Chicana Latina Foundation seeks to empower Latinas in higher education and the workplace by providing scholarships for Latinas, mentorship, skill-building workshops, and a community for future and present Latina leaders.

Latin American Canadian Art Projects
100-39 Queens Quay East
Toronto, ON M5E 0A5
Canada
(416) 654-7787
Website: http://lacap.ca/home
Facebook: @LACAParts
This organization promotes Latin American art in Canada.

League of United Latin American Citizens (LULAC)
National Office
1133 19th Street NW, Suite 1000
Washington, DC 20036
(202) 833-6130
Website: http://lulac.org
Facebook: @lulac.national.dc
Twitter: @lulac
LULAC is the largest and oldest organization for Latinos in the United States. They provide educational programs and scholarships for students, promote political engagement through citizenship and voter registration drives, and provide employment opportunities and literacy training.

MANA
1140 19th Street NW, Suite 550
Washington, DC 20036
(202) 525-5113
Website: https://www.hermana.org
Facebook and Twitter: @MANANational
MANA is a national Latina organization that represents the
    interests of Latina women, youth, and families. They
    advocate for immigration reform, financial literacy, civil
    rights, and educational opportunities.

Mexican American Legal Defense and Educational Fund
    (MALDEF)
National Headquarters
634 South Spring Street
Los Angeles, CA 90014
(213) 629-2512
Website: http://www.maldef.org/index.html
Facebook: @MALDEF
MALDEF promotes social change through advocacy and
    community education and litigation in education,
    employment, immigrant rights, and political access.

Unidos US
1126 16th Street NW, Suite 600
Washington, DC 20036
(202) 785-1670
Website: https://www.unidosus.org

Facebook: @weareunidosus
Twitter: @Weareunidosus
Unidos US seeks to enrich the Latino community through
   research, analysis, and political engagement.

United Farm Workers of America
National Headquarters
29700 Woodford-Tehachapi Road
P.O. Box 62
Keene, CA 93531
(661) 823-6151
Website: http://ufw.org
Facebook: @unitedfarmworkers
Twitter: @UFWupdates
Founded as the National Farm Workers Association by
   Cesar Chavez and Dolores Huerta in 1962, today the
   UFW continues to advocate for the fair treatment of
   farm workers.

Alire Sáenz, Benjamin. *The Inexplicable Logic of My Life*. New York, NY: Clarion Books, 2017.

Coleman, Miriam. *The Culture and Crafts of Mexico*. New York, NY: Rosen Publishing, 2016.

Conkling, Winifred. *Sylvia & Aki*. New York, NY: Yearling, 2013.

Foley, Neil. *Mexicans in the Making of America*. Cambridge, MA: The Belknap Press of Harvard University Press, 2014.

Giff, Patricia Reilly. *Until I Find Julian*. New York, NY: Yearling, 2015.

Honders, Christine. *Mexican American Civil Rights Movement*. New York, NY: Rosen Publishing, 2017.

Luiselli, Valeria. *Tell Me How It Ends: An Essay in Forty Questions*. Minneapolis, MN: Coffee House Press, 2017. Malavé, Idelisse. *Latino Stats: American Hispanics by the Numbers*. New York, NY: The New Press, 2015.

Mooney, Carla. *La Economía (The Economy of Latin America)*. New York, NY: Rosen Publishing, 2018.

Stanley, Joseph. *The Expansion of the United States: Florida, Alaska, Gadsden Purchase, and Mexican Cession*. New York, NY: Rosen Publishing, 2017.

VISA

UNITED STAT

BIBLIOGRAPHY

Acuña, Rodolfo. *The Making of Chicana/o Studies in the Trenches of Academe.* New Brunswick, NJ: Rutgers University Press, 2011.

Balderrama, Francisco. "America's Forgotten History Of Mexican-American 'Repatriation.'" By Terry Gross, NPR *Fresh Air*, September 10, 2015. http://www.npr.org/2015/09/10/439114563/americas-forgotten-history-of-mexican-american-repatriation.

Blackwell, Maylei. *Chicana Power! Contested Histories of Feminism in the Chicano Movement.* Austin, TX: University of Texas Press, 2011.

Boullosa, Carmen, and Mike Wallace. "How the Cartels Were Born." *Jacobin*, March 16, 2015. http://www.jacobinmag.com/2015/03/mexico-drug-cartel-neoliberalism.

Con Davis-Undiano, Robert. *Mestizos Come Home! Making and Claiming Mexican American Identity.* Norman, OK: University of Oklahoma Press, 2017.

Durand, Jorge, and Douglas S. Massey. *Crossing the Border: Research from the Mexican Migration Project.* New York, NY: Russell Sage Foundation, 2006.

García, Juan Ramón. *Mexican Americans in the 1990s: Politics, Policies, and Perceptions. Perspectives in Mexican American Studies*, Vol. 6 (1997). Tucson, AZ: Mexican American Studies & Research Center, University of Arizona.

García, Juan Ramón. *Operation Wetback: The Mass Deportation of Mexican Undocumented Workers in 1954.* Westport, CT: Greenwood Press, 1980.

Hanson, Sandra L., and John Kenneth White. *The Latino/a American Dream*. College Station, TX: Texas A&M University Press, 2016.

Kopan, Tal. "What Donald Trump Has Said About Mexico and Vice Versa." CNN, August 31, 2016. http://www.cnn.com/2016/08/31/politics/donald-trump-mexico-statements/index.html.

Meier, Matt S., and Feliciano Ribera. *Mexican Americans, American Mexicans: From Conquistadors to Chicanos*. New York, NY: Hill & Wang, 1993.

Mitchell, Faith, and Marta Tienda. *Multiple Origins, Uncertain Destinies: Hispanics and the American Future*. Washington, DC: National Academies Press, 2006.

Murphy, Douglas A. *Two Armies on the Rio Grande: The First Campaign of the US-Mexican War*. College Station, TX: Texas A&M University Press, 2015.

Neumann, Caryn E., and Tammy S. Allen. *Latino History Day by Day: A Reference Guide to Events*. Santa Barbara, CA: Greenwood, 2013.

Pimentel, Octavio. *Historias de Éxito Within Mexican Communities: Silenced Voices*. New York, NY: Palgrave MacMillan, 2015.

Rivera, John-Michael. *The Emergence of Mexican America*. New York, NY: New York University Press, 2006.

Rumbaut, Rubén G. "The Making of a People." In *Hispanics and the Future of America,* edited by Marta Tienda and Faith Mitchell as part of the National Research Council Panel on Hispanics in the United States. Washington,

DC: The National Academies Press, 2006. https://www.
ncbi.nlm.nih.gov/books/NBK19896.

Saenz, Rogelio, and Maria Christina Morales. *Latinos in the
United States: Diversity and Change*. Cambridge, UK:
Polity Press, 2015.

Wagenen, Michael Van. *Enduring Legacies of the U.S./
Mexican War*. Amherst, MA: University of Massachusetts
Press, 2012.

INDEX

ABOUT THE AUTHOR

Ash Imery-Garcia is a second-generation Mexican American from San Antonio, Texas. She comes from a family of migrant workers, coyotes, and hardworking immigrant entrepreneurs. She received her bachelor's degree in English literature from New York University.

PHOTO CREDITS

Cover, p. 3 Gary Conner/Photolibrary/Getty Images; pp. 6–7 PHAS/Universal Images Group/Getty Images; p. 13 DEA Picture Library/De Agostini/Getty Images; p. 15 GraphicaArtis/Archive Photos/Getty Images; p. 16 National Archives; p. 21 Hulton Deutsch/Corbis Historical/Getty Images; p. 25 Paul Levine /New York Daily News/Getty Images; pp. 27, 35, 41 Bettmann /Getty Images; p. 33 Ira Gay Sealy/Denver Post/Getty Images; p. 43 © AP Images; p. 46 Felipe Davalos/NATIONAL GEOGRAPHIC IMAGE COLLECTION/Getty Images; p. 48 Arthur Schatz /The LIFE Picture Collection/Getty Images; p. 51 Michael S. Lewis/NATIONAL GEOGRAPHIC IMAGE COLLECTION /Getty Images; p. 53 Gulbenk/Wikimedia Commons /FILE: U.S. Citizenship and Immigration Service.jpg/CC BY 3.0; p. 56 John Moore/Getty Images; p. 59 Alex Wong /Getty Images; p. 63 Zach Gibson/Getty Images; interior pages designs (portrait collage) Ollyy/Shutterstock.com, (USA stamp) ducu59us/Shutterstock.com, (fingerprint) Rigamondis /Shutterstock.com, (brochure) Konstanin L/Shutterstock.com, (visa) Sergiy Palamarchuk/Shutterstock.com.

Design: Nelson Sá; Layout: Nicole Russo-Duca; Photo Researcher: Karen Huang

VISA

UNITED STAT